MW00944335

WEBSITE:	
USERNAME:	
PASSWORD:	
EMAIL ADDRESS:	
NOTES/HINTS:	

WEBSITE:	
USERNAME:	
PASSWORD:	
EMAIL ADDRESS:	
NOTES/HINTS:	

WEBSITE:	
USERNAME:	
PASSWORD:	
EMAIL ADDRESS:	
NOTES/HINTS:	

WEBSITE:	
USERNAME:	
PASSWORD:	
EMAIL ADDRESS:	
NOTES/HINTS:	

WEBSITE:	
USERNAME:	
PASSWORD:	
EMAIL ADDRESS:	
NOTES/HINTS:	

WEBSITE:	
USERNAME:	
PASSWORD:	
EMAIL ADDRESS:	
NOTES/HINTS:	

WEBSITE:	
USERNAME:	
PASSWORD:	
EMAIL ADDRESS:	
NOTES/HINTS:	

WEBSITE:	
USERNAME:	
PASSWORD:	
EMAIL ADDRESS:	
NOTES/HINTS:	

WEBSITE:	
USERNAME:	
PASSWORD:	
EMAIL ADDRESS:	
NOTES/HINTS:	

WEBSITE:	
USERNAME:	
PASSWORD:	
EMAIL ADDRESS:	
NOTES/HINTS:	

WEBSITE:	
USERNAME:	
PASSWORD:	
EMAIL ADDRESS:	
NOTES/HINTS:	

WEBSITE:	
USERNAME:	
PASSWORD:	
EMAIL ADDRESS:	
NOTES/HINTS:	

WEBSITE:	
USERNAME:	
PASSWORD:	
EMAIL ADDRESS:	
NOTES/HINTS:	

WEBSITE:	
USERNAME:	
PASSWORD:	
EMAIL ADDRESS:	
NOTES/HINTS:	

WEBSITE:	
USERNAME:	
PASSWORD:	
EMAIL ADDRESS:	
NOTES/HINTS:	

WEBSITE:	
USERNAME:	
PASSWORD:	
EMAIL ADDRESS:	
NOTES/HINTS:	

WEBSITE:	
USERNAME:	
PASSWORD:	
EMAIL ADDRESS:	
NOTES/HINTS:	

WEBSITE:	
USERNAME:	
PASSWORD:	
EMAIL ADDRESS:	
NOTES/HINTS:	

WEBSITE:	
USERNAME:	
PASSWORD:	
EMAIL ADDRESS:	
NOTES/HINTS:	

WEBSITE:	
USERNAME:	
PASSWORD:	
EMAIL ADDRESS:	
NOTES/HINTS:	

WEBSITE:	
USERNAME:	
PASSWORD:	
EMAIL ADDRESS:	
NOTES/HINTS:	

WEBSITE:	
USERNAME:	
PASSWORD:	
EMAIL ADDRESS:	
NOTES/HINTS:	

WEBSITE:	
USERNAME:	
PASSWORD:	
EMAIL ADDRESS:	
NOTES/HINTS:	

WEBSITE:	
USERNAME:	
PASSWORD:	
EMAIL ADDRESS:	
NOTES/HINTS:	

WEBSITE:	
USERNAME:	
PASSWORD:	
EMAIL ADDRESS:	
NOTES/HINTS:	

WEBSITE:	
USERNAME:	
PASSWORD:	
EMAIL ADDRESS:	
NOTES/HINTS:	

WEBSITE:	
USERNAME:	
PASSWORD:	
EMAIL ADDRESS:	
NOTES/HINTS:	

WEBSITE:	
USERNAME:	
PASSWORD:	
EMAIL ADDRESS:	
NOTES/HINTS:	

WEBSITE:	
USERNAME:	
PASSWORD:	
EMAIL ADDRESS:	
NOTES/HINTS:	

WEBSITE:	
USERNAME:	
PASSWORD:	
EMAIL ADDRESS:	
NOTES/HINTS:	

WEBSITE:	
USERNAME:	
PASSWORD:	
EMAIL ADDRESS:	
NOTES/HINTS:	

WEBSITE:	
USERNAME:	
PASSWORD:	
EMAIL ADDRESS:	
NOTES/HINTS:	

WEBSITE:	
USERNAME:	
PASSWORD:	
EMAIL ADDRESS:	
NOTES/HINTS:	

WEBSITE:	
USERNAME:	
PASSWORD:	
EMAIL ADDRESS:	
NOTES/HINTS:	

WEBSITE:	
USERNAME:	
PASSWORD:	
EMAIL ADDRESS:	
NOTES/HINTS:	

WEBSITE:	
USERNAME:	
PASSWORD:	
EMAIL ADDRESS:	
NOTES/HINTS:	

WEBSITE:	
USERNAME:	
PASSWORD:	
EMAIL ADDRESS:	
NOTES/HINTS:	

WEBSITE:	
USERNAME:	
PASSWORD:	
EMAIL ADDRESS:	
NOTES/HINTS:	

WEBSITE:	
USERNAME:	
PASSWORD:	
EMAIL ADDRESS:	
NOTES/HINTS:	

WEBSITE:	
USERNAME:	
PASSWORD:	
EMAIL ADDRESS:	
NOTES/HINTS:	

WEBSITE:	
USERNAME:	
PASSWORD:	
EMAIL ADDRESS:	
NOTES/HINTS:	

WEBSITE:	
USERNAME:	
PASSWORD:	
EMAIL ADDRESS:	
NOTES/HINTS:	

WEBSITE:	
USERNAME:	
PASSWORD:	
EMAIL ADDRESS:	
NOTES/HINTS:	

WEBSITE:	
USERNAME:	
PASSWORD:	
EMAIL ADDRESS:	
NOTES/HINTS:	

WEBSITE:	
USERNAME:	
PASSWORD:	
EMAIL ADDRESS:	
NOTES/HINTS:	

WEBSITE:	
USERNAME:	
PASSWORD:	
EMAIL ADDRESS:	
NOTES/HINTS:	

WEBSITE:	
USERNAME:	
PASSWORD:	
EMAIL ADDRESS:	
NOTES/HINTS:	

WEBSITE:	
USERNAME:	
PASSWORD:	
EMAIL ADDRESS:	
NOTES/HINTS:	

WEBSITE:	
USERNAME:	
PASSWORD:	
EMAIL ADDRESS:	
NOTES/HINTS:	

WEBSITE:	
USERNAME:	
PASSWORD:	
EMAIL ADDRESS:	
NOTES/HINTS:	

WEBSITE:	
USERNAME:	
PASSWORD:	
EMAIL ADDRESS:	
NOTES/HINTS:	

WEBSITE:	
USERNAME:	
PASSWORD:	
EMAIL ADDRESS:	
NOTES/HINTS:	

WEBSITE:	
USERNAME:	
PASSWORD:	
EMAIL ADDRESS:	
NOTES/HINTS:	

WEBSITE:	
USERNAME:	
PASSWORD:	
EMAIL ADDRESS:	
NOTES/HINTS:	

WEBSITE:	
USERNAME:	
PASSWORD:	
EMAIL ADDRESS:	
NOTES/HINTS:	

WEBSITE:	
USERNAME:	
PASSWORD:	
EMAIL ADDRESS:	
NOTES/HINTS:	

WEBSITE:	
USERNAME:	
PASSWORD:	
EMAIL ADDRESS:	
NOTES/HINTS:	

WEBSITE:	
USERNAME:	
PASSWORD:	
EMAIL ADDRESS:	
NOTES/HINTS:	

WEBSITE:	
USERNAME:	
PASSWORD:	
EMAIL ADDRESS:	
NOTES/HINTS:	

WEBSITE:	
USERNAME:	
PASSWORD:	
EMAIL ADDRESS:	
NOTES/HINTS:	

WEBSITE:	
USERNAME:	
PASSWORD:	
EMAIL ADDRESS:	
NOTES/HINTS:	

WEBSITE:	
USERNAME:	
PASSWORD:	
EMAIL ADDRESS:	
NOTES/HINTS:	

WEBSITE:	
USERNAME:	
PASSWORD:	
EMAIL ADDRESS:	
NOTES/HINTS:	

WEBSITE:	
USERNAME:	
PASSWORD:	
EMAIL ADDRESS:	
NOTES/HINTS:	

WEBSITE:	
USERNAME:	
PASSWORD:	
EMAIL ADDRESS:	
NOTES/HINTS:	

WEBSITE:	
USERNAME:	
PASSWORD:	
EMAIL ADDRESS:	
NOTES/HINTS:	

WEBSITE:	
USERNAME:	
PASSWORD:	
EMAIL ADDRESS:	
NOTES/HINTS:	

WEBSITE:	
USERNAME:	
PASSWORD:	
EMAIL ADDRESS:	
NOTES/HINTS:	

WEBSITE:	
USERNAME:	
PASSWORD:	
EMAIL ADDRESS:	
NOTES/HINTS:	

WEBSITE:	
USERNAME:	
PASSWORD:	
EMAIL ADDRESS:	
NOTES/HINTS:	

WEBSITE:	
USERNAME:	
PASSWORD:	
EMAIL ADDRESS:	
NOTES/HINTS:	

WEBSITE:	
USERNAME:	
PASSWORD:	
EMAIL ADDRESS:	
NOTES/HINTS:	

WEBSITE:	
USERNAME:	
PASSWORD:	
EMAIL ADDRESS:	
NOTES/HINTS:	

WEBSITE:	
USERNAME:	
PASSWORD:	
EMAIL ADDRESS:	
NOTES/HINTS:	

WEBSITE:	
USERNAME:	
PASSWORD:	
EMAIL ADDRESS:	
NOTES/HINTS:	

WEBSITE:	
USERNAME:	
PASSWORD:	
EMAIL ADDRESS:	
NOTES/HINTS:	

WEBSITE:	
USERNAME:	
PASSWORD:	
EMAIL ADDRESS:	
NOTES/HINTS:	

WEBSITE:	
USERNAME:	
PASSWORD:	
EMAIL ADDRESS:	
NOTES/HINTS:	

WEBSITE:	
USERNAME:	
PASSWORD:	
EMAIL ADDRESS:	
NOTES/HINTS:	

WEBSITE:	
USERNAME:	
PASSWORD:	
EMAIL ADDRESS:	
NOTES/HINTS:	

WEBSITE:	
USERNAME:	
PASSWORD:	
EMAIL ADDRESS:	
NOTES/HINTS:	

WEBSITE:	
USERNAME:	
PASSWORD:	
EMAIL ADDRESS:	
NOTES/HINTS:	

WEBSITE:	
USERNAME:	
PASSWORD:	
EMAIL ADDRESS:	
NOTES/HINTS:	

WEBSITE:	
USERNAME:	
PASSWORD:	
EMAIL ADDRESS:	
NOTES/HINTS:	

WEBSITE:	
USERNAME:	
PASSWORD:	
EMAIL ADDRESS:	
NOTES/HINTS:	

WEBSITE:	
USERNAME:	
PASSWORD:	
EMAIL ADDRESS:	
NOTES/HINTS:	

WEBSITE:	
USERNAME:	
PASSWORD:	
EMAIL ADDRESS:	
NOTES/HINTS:	

WEBSITE:	
USERNAME:	
PASSWORD:	
EMAIL ADDRESS:	
NOTES/HINTS:	

WEBSITE:	
USERNAME:	
PASSWORD:	
EMAIL ADDRESS:	
NOTES/HINTS:	

WEBSITE:	
USERNAME:	
PASSWORD:	
EMAIL ADDRESS:	
NOTES/HINTS:	

WEBSITE:	
USERNAME:	
PASSWORD:	
EMAIL ADDRESS:	
NOTES/HINTS:	

WEBSITE:	
USERNAME:	
PASSWORD:	
EMAIL ADDRESS:	
NOTES/HINTS:	

WEBSITE:	
USERNAME:	
PASSWORD:	
EMAIL ADDRESS:	
NOTES/HINTS:	

WEBSITE:	
USERNAME:	
PASSWORD:	
EMAIL ADDRESS:	
NOTES/HINTS:	

WEBSITE:	
USERNAME:	
PASSWORD:	
EMAIL ADDRESS:	
NOTES/HINTS:	

WEBSITE:	
USERNAME:	
PASSWORD:	
EMAIL ADDRESS:	
NOTES/HINTS:	

WEBSITE:	
USERNAME:	
PASSWORD:	
EMAIL ADDRESS:	
NOTES/HINTS:	

WEBSITE:	
USERNAME:	
PASSWORD:	
EMAIL ADDRESS:	
NOTES/HINTS:	

WEBSITE:	
USERNAME:	
PASSWORD:	
EMAIL ADDRESS:	
NOTES/HINTS:	

WEBSITE:	
USERNAME:	
PASSWORD:	
EMAIL ADDRESS:	
NOTES/HINTS:	

WEBSITE:	
USERNAME:	
PASSWORD:	
EMAIL ADDRESS:	
NOTES/HINTS:	

WEBSITE:	
USERNAME:	
PASSWORD:	
EMAIL ADDRESS:	
NOTES/HINTS:	

WEBSITE:	
USERNAME:	
PASSWORD:	
EMAIL ADDRESS:	
NOTES/HINTS:	

WEBSITE:	
USERNAME:	
PASSWORD:	
EMAIL ADDRESS:	
NOTES/HINTS:	

WEBSITE:	
USERNAME:	
PASSWORD:	
EMAIL ADDRESS:	
NOTES/HINTS:	

WEBSITE:	
USERNAME:	
PASSWORD:	
EMAIL ADDRESS:	
NOTES/HINTS:	

WEBSITE:	
USERNAME:	
PASSWORD:	
EMAIL ADDRESS:	
NOTES/HINTS:	

WEBSITE:	
USERNAME:	
PASSWORD:	
EMAIL ADDRESS:	
NOTES/HINTS:	

WEBSITE:	
USERNAME:	
PASSWORD:	
EMAIL ADDRESS:	
NOTES/HINTS:	

WEBSITE:	
USERNAME:	
PASSWORD:	
EMAIL ADDRESS:	
NOTES/HINTS:	

WEBSITE:	
USERNAME:	
PASSWORD:	
EMAIL ADDRESS:	
NOTES/HINTS:	

WEBSITE:	
USERNAME:	
PASSWORD:	
EMAIL ADDRESS:	
NOTES/HINTS:	

WEBSITE:	
USERNAME:	
PASSWORD:	
EMAIL ADDRESS:	
NOTES/HINTS:	

WEBSITE:	
USERNAME:	
PASSWORD:	
EMAIL ADDRESS:	
NOTES/HINTS:	

WEBSITE:	
USERNAME:	
PASSWORD:	
EMAIL ADDRESS:	
NOTES/HINTS:	

WEBSITE:	
USERNAME:	
PASSWORD:	
EMAIL ADDRESS:	
NOTES/HINTS:	

WEBSITE:	
USERNAME:	
PASSWORD:	
EMAIL ADDRESS:	
NOTES/HINTS:	

WEBSITE:	
USERNAME:	
PASSWORD:	
EMAIL ADDRESS:	
NOTES/HINTS:	

WEBSITE:	
USERNAME:	
PASSWORD:	
EMAIL ADDRESS:	
NOTES/HINTS:	

WEBSITE:	
USERNAME:	
PASSWORD:	
EMAIL ADDRESS:	
NOTES/HINTS:	

WEBSITE:	
USERNAME:	
PASSWORD:	
EMAIL ADDRESS:	
NOTES/HINTS:	

WEBSITE:	
USERNAME:	
PASSWORD:	
EMAIL ADDRESS:	
NOTES/HINTS:	

WEBSITE:	
USERNAME:	
PASSWORD:	
EMAIL ADDRESS:	
NOTES/HINTS:	

WEBSITE:	
USERNAME:	
PASSWORD:	
EMAIL ADDRESS:	
NOTES/HINTS:	

WEBSITE:	
USERNAME:	
PASSWORD:	
EMAIL ADDRESS:	
NOTES/HINTS:	

WEBSITE:	
USERNAME:	
PASSWORD:	
EMAIL ADDRESS:	
NOTES/HINTS:	

WEBSITE:	
USERNAME:	
PASSWORD:	
EMAIL ADDRESS:	
NOTES/HINTS:	

WEBSITE:	
USERNAME:	
PASSWORD:	
EMAIL ADDRESS:	
NOTES/HINTS:	

WEBSITE:	
USERNAME:	
PASSWORD:	
EMAIL ADDRESS:	
NOTES/HINTS:	

WEBSITE:	
USERNAME:	
PASSWORD:	
EMAIL ADDRESS:	
NOTES/HINTS:	

WEBSITE:	
USERNAME:	
PASSWORD:	
EMAIL ADDRESS:	
NOTES/HINTS:	

WEBSITE:	
USERNAME:	
PASSWORD:	
EMAIL ADDRESS:	
NOTES/HINTS:	

WEBSITE:	
USERNAME:	
PASSWORD:	
EMAIL ADDRESS:	
NOTES/HINTS:	

WEBSITE:	
USERNAME:	
PASSWORD:	
EMAIL ADDRESS:	
NOTES/HINTS:	

WEBSITE:	
USERNAME:	
PASSWORD:	
EMAIL ADDRESS:	
NOTES/HINTS:	

WEBSITE:	
USERNAME:	
PASSWORD:	
EMAIL ADDRESS:	
NOTES/HINTS:	

WEBSITE:	
USERNAME:	
PASSWORD:	
EMAIL ADDRESS:	
NOTES/HINTS:	

WEBSITE:	
USERNAME:	
PASSWORD:	
EMAIL ADDRESS:	
NOTES/HINTS:	

WEBSITE:	
USERNAME:	
PASSWORD:	
EMAIL ADDRESS:	
NOTES/HINTS:	

WEBSITE:	
USERNAME:	
PASSWORD:	
EMAIL ADDRESS:	
NOTES/HINTS:	

WEBSITE:	
USERNAME:	
PASSWORD:	
EMAIL ADDRESS:	
NOTES/HINTS:	

WEBSITE:	
USERNAME:	
PASSWORD:	
EMAIL ADDRESS:	
NOTES/HINTS:	

WEBSITE:	
USERNAME:	
PASSWORD:	
EMAIL ADDRESS:	
NOTES/HINTS:	

WEBSITE:	
USERNAME:	
PASSWORD:	
EMAIL ADDRESS:	
NOTES/HINTS:	

WEBSITE:	
USERNAME:	
PASSWORD:	
EMAIL ADDRESS:	
NOTES/HINTS:	

WEBSITE:	
USERNAME:	
PASSWORD:	
EMAIL ADDRESS:	
NOTES/HINTS:	

WEBSITE:	
USERNAME:	
PASSWORD:	
EMAIL ADDRESS:	
NOTES/HINTS:	

WEBSITE:	
USERNAME:	
PASSWORD:	
EMAIL ADDRESS:	
NOTES/HINTS:	

WEBSITE:	
USERNAME:	
PASSWORD:	
EMAIL ADDRESS:	
NOTES/HINTS:	

WEBSITE:	
USERNAME:	
PASSWORD:	
EMAIL ADDRESS:	
NOTES/HINTS:	

WEBSITE:	
USERNAME:	
PASSWORD:	
EMAIL ADDRESS:	
NOTES/HINTS:	

WEBSITE:	
USERNAME:	
PASSWORD:	
EMAIL ADDRESS:	
NOTES/HINTS:	

WEBSITE:	
USERNAME:	
PASSWORD:	
EMAIL ADDRESS:	
NOTES/HINTS:	

WEBSITE:	
USERNAME:	
PASSWORD:	
EMAIL ADDRESS:	
NOTES/HINTS:	

WEBSITE:	
USERNAME:	
PASSWORD:	
EMAIL ADDRESS:	
NOTES/HINTS:	

WEBSITE:	
USERNAME:	
PASSWORD:	
EMAIL ADDRESS:	
NOTES/HINTS:	

WEBSITE:	
USERNAME:	
PASSWORD:	
EMAIL ADDRESS:	
NOTES/HINTS:	

WEBSITE:	
USERNAME:	
PASSWORD:	
EMAIL ADDRESS:	
NOTES/HINTS:	

WEBSITE:	
USERNAME:	
PASSWORD:	
EMAIL ADDRESS:	
NOTES/HINTS:	

WEBSITE:	
USERNAME:	
PASSWORD:	
EMAIL ADDRESS:	
NOTES/HINTS:	

WEBSITE:	
USERNAME:	
PASSWORD:	
EMAIL ADDRESS:	
NOTES/HINTS:	

WEBSITE:	
USERNAME:	
PASSWORD:	
EMAIL ADDRESS:	
NOTES/HINTS:	

WEBSITE:	
USERNAME:	
PASSWORD:	
EMAIL ADDRESS:	
NOTES/HINTS:	

WEBSITE:	
USERNAME:	
PASSWORD:	
EMAIL ADDRESS:	
NOTES/HINTS:	

WEBSITE:	
USERNAME:	
PASSWORD:	
EMAIL ADDRESS:	
NOTES/HINTS:	

WEBSITE:	
USERNAME:	
PASSWORD:	
EMAIL ADDRESS:	
NOTES/HINTS:	

WEBSITE:	
USERNAME:	
PASSWORD:	
EMAIL ADDRESS:	
NOTES/HINTS:	

WEBSITE:	
USERNAME:	
PASSWORD:	
EMAIL ADDRESS:	
NOTES/HINTS:	

WEBSITE:	
USERNAME:	
PASSWORD:	
EMAIL ADDRESS:	
NOTES/HINTS:	

WEBSITE:	
USERNAME:	
PASSWORD:	
EMAIL ADDRESS:	
NOTES/HINTS:	

WEBSITE:	
USERNAME:	
PASSWORD:	
EMAIL ADDRESS:	
NOTES/HINTS:	

WEBSITE:	
USERNAME:	
PASSWORD:	
EMAIL ADDRESS:	
NOTES/HINTS:	

WEBSITE:	
USERNAME:	
PASSWORD:	
EMAIL ADDRESS:	
NOTES/HINTS:	

WEBSITE:	
USERNAME:	
PASSWORD:	
EMAIL ADDRESS:	
NOTES/HINTS:	

WEBSITE:	
USERNAME:	
PASSWORD:	
EMAIL ADDRESS:	
NOTES/HINTS:	

WEBSITE:	
USERNAME:	
PASSWORD:	
EMAIL ADDRESS:	
NOTES/HINTS:	

WEBSITE:	
USERNAME:	
PASSWORD:	
EMAIL ADDRESS:	
NOTES/HINTS:	

WEBSITE:	
USERNAME:	
PASSWORD:	
EMAIL ADDRESS:	
NOTES/HINTS:	

WEBSITE:	
USERNAME:	
PASSWORD:	
EMAIL ADDRESS:	
NOTES/HINTS:	

WEBSITE:	
USERNAME:	
PASSWORD:	
EMAIL ADDRESS:	
NOTES/HINTS:	

WEBSITE:	
USERNAME:	
PASSWORD:	
EMAIL ADDRESS:	
NOTES/HINTS:	

WEBSITE:	
USERNAME:	
PASSWORD:	
EMAIL ADDRESS:	
NOTES/HINTS:	

WEBSITE:	
USERNAME:	
PASSWORD:	
EMAIL ADDRESS:	
NOTES/HINTS:	

WEBSITE:	
USERNAME:	
PASSWORD:	
EMAIL ADDRESS:	
NOTES/HINTS:	

WEBSITE:	
USERNAME:	
PASSWORD:	
EMAIL ADDRESS:	
NOTES/HINTS:	

WEBSITE:	
USERNAME:	
PASSWORD:	
EMAIL ADDRESS:	
NOTES/HINTS:	

WEBSITE:	
USERNAME:	
PASSWORD:	
EMAIL ADDRESS:	
NOTES/HINTS:	

WEBSITE:	
USERNAME:	
PASSWORD:	
EMAIL ADDRESS:	
NOTES/HINTS:	

WEBSITE:	
USERNAME:	
PASSWORD:	
EMAIL ADDRESS:	
NOTES/HINTS:	

WEBSITE:	
USERNAME:	
PASSWORD:	
EMAIL ADDRESS:	
NOTES/HINTS:	

WEBSITE:	
USERNAME:	
PASSWORD:	
EMAIL ADDRESS:	
NOTES/HINTS:	

WEBSITE:	
USERNAME:	
PASSWORD:	
EMAIL ADDRESS:	
NOTES/HINTS:	

WEBSITE:	
USERNAME:	
PASSWORD:	
EMAIL ADDRESS:	
NOTES/HINTS:	

WEBSITE:	
USERNAME:	
PASSWORD:	
EMAIL ADDRESS:	
NOTES/HINTS:	

WEBSITE:	
USERNAME:	
PASSWORD:	
EMAIL ADDRESS:	
NOTES/HINTS:	

WEBSITE:	
USERNAME:	
PASSWORD:	
EMAIL ADDRESS:	
NOTES/HINTS:	

WEBSITE:	
USERNAME:	
PASSWORD:	
EMAIL ADDRESS:	
NOTES/HINTS:	

WEBSITE:	
USERNAME:	
PASSWORD:	
EMAIL ADDRESS:	
NOTES/HINTS:	

WEBSITE:	
USERNAME:	
PASSWORD:	
EMAIL ADDRESS:	
NOTES/HINTS:	

WEBSITE:	
USERNAME:	
PASSWORD:	
EMAIL ADDRESS:	
NOTES/HINTS:	

WEBSITE:	
USERNAME:	
PASSWORD:	
EMAIL ADDRESS:	
NOTES/HINTS:	

WEBSITE:	
USERNAME:	
PASSWORD:	
EMAIL ADDRESS:	
NOTES/HINTS:	

WEBSITE:	
USERNAME:	
PASSWORD:	
EMAIL ADDRESS:	
NOTES/HINTS:	

WEBSITE:	
USERNAME:	
PASSWORD:	
EMAIL ADDRESS:	
NOTES/HINTS:	

WEBSITE:	
USERNAME:	
PASSWORD:	
EMAIL ADDRESS:	
NOTES/HINTS:	

WEBSITE:	
USERNAME:	
PASSWORD:	
EMAIL ADDRESS:	
NOTES/HINTS:	

WEBSITE:	
USERNAME:	
PASSWORD:	
EMAIL ADDRESS:	
NOTES/HINTS:	

WEBSITE:	
USERNAME:	
PASSWORD:	
EMAIL ADDRESS:	
NOTES/HINTS:	

NOTES

NOTES

NOTES

NOTES

NOTES

Made in the USA
San Bernardino, CA
04 December 2015